HOMES FOR THE COUNTRY

Also by RA Briggs in JM Classic Editions
Bungalows and Country Residences

HOMES FOR THE COUNTRY

A SERIES OF DESIGNS AND EXAMPLES OF
EXECUTED WORKS, WITH PLANS OF EACH

ILLUSTRATED ON FIFTY-FOUR PLATES

BY

R. A. BRIGGS, Architect, F.R.I.B.A.

(Soane Medallist)

AUTHOR OF "BUNGALOWS AND COUNTRY RESIDENCES"

CLASSIC EDITIONS

This edition digitally re-mastered and
published by JM Classic Editions © 2007
Original text © RA Briggs 1909

ISBN 978-1-905217-70-0

All rights reserved. No part of this book subject
to copyright may be reproduced in any form or
by any means without prior permission in writing
from the publisher.

PREFACE.

THE pleasing fact that my book entitled "Bungalows and Country Residences" is now running through its fifth edition has led me to cherish the hope that a similar volume, showing a still greater variety of designs for Country Houses, will be of interest to that numerous class who contemplate building a house, but are unable to decide in what form their ideas may be carried out. I trust that, after turning over these pages, those troubled by this uncertainty may be able the more easily to come to some conclusion as to which style of house and what arrangement of plan will most readily fit in with their requirements and preconceptions.

I have attempted to give as great a diversity of styles and plans as possible, selecting from my sketches made during the last three years those I think will most advantageously fulfil this object. In nearly all cases, estimates have already been given or prepared for the erection of the houses illustrated.

I have purposely refrained from including any houses designed in the phase known as "L'Art nouveau," now practised by some architects on the Continent, as I regard it as but a passing mode, based on non-constructive and inartistic principles.

Although in this book will be found some examples of large and of moderate-sized houses, there are many of a much smaller class, suitable for people living in towns, whose means are not sufficient for keeping up a large Country House in addition to their Town House, but are ample enough to extend to a small Bungalow-House in the country. Here the children can be sent for a change, and here paterfamilias, unable to live in the country, may, after days of toil, fly to spend his week-ends, turned thereto perhaps by the words of Cowley:—

> "Who that has reason and smell
> Would not among Roses and Jesamine dwell,
> Rather then all his spirits choak
> With exhalations of dust and smoak,
> And all the uncleanness which does drown
> In pestilential clouds a populous town."

Here too he can pass his vacations in the bosom of his family, away from the grime and bustle of the city, happy in the thought that his drains are unlike those of some of the lodging houses of some of the fashionable seaside resorts, and with no fears that the outcome of his holidays will be typhoid or other kindred troubles.

In this grey climate of ours, where we have more mists and clouds than sunshine, we must take good care that we plan our houses, so that, if possible, at any rate during one portion of the day, we allow the sun's rays to enter our rooms. A room that never has the sun in it is always a dull room, and as scientists tell us, sunlight is the great destroyer of microbes.

It is generally of advantage to have the Entrance of the house on the north side, so that as many of the Living-rooms as possible may face the south. The Morning-room or Dining-room can face the south and east, and the Drawing-room—a room used mostly in the afternoon and evening—can face the south and west. The Kitchen-offices can, and the Larder must, face the north. The Larder should be entered from the Scullery, so as to be near the Kitchen, but separated from its heat. The Pantry should be near the Entrance, near the Dining-room, and near the Kitchen. A Sitting-room-hall is a very useful arrangement, as it can be used for a number of purposes. It also does away with a lot of passages, which except for the purpose of giving access to rooms are waste space. Nothing gives a better impression, on entering a house, than to find oneself in a good-sized, well-ventilated and lighted Hall.

A few suggestions as to the construction of our houses will, I trust, be useful to the uninitiated. We are, to a great extent, bound by the materials we find in the locality in which we build, although cheaper transport now-a-days has to some extent modified this. In a stone district we should build our walls with stone, backing them with bricks where procurable, when the stone is of a somewhat porous nature. Where there are tiles, let us have tiles for the roof, and where there are slates, let us have slates. I am inclined to avoid "half timber" work. In most districts it must be "planted on" to a brick wall, to comply with the bye-laws of the local authorities, and therefore, being a sham, is contrary to the canons of good taste. "Rough-cast," where economy is an essential, is a natural and thoroughly artistic means of treating a wall in exposed positions, to make it a good dry wall and to keep out the damp. If a brick face is desired, walls with a cavity can be built in exposed positions. Felt should always be put to roofs under the slates or tiles. It keeps the rooms under the roof dry, cool in summer, and warm in winter. But whatever we do, let us have the best materials procurable and good honest work. Swift gives us good advice in his poem on the true basis of happiness in married life ("Strephon and Chloë"):—

> "A prudent builder should forecast
> How long the stuff is like to last,
> And carefully observe the ground,
> To build on some foundations sound.
> What House when its materials crumble
> Must not inevitably tumble?
> What edifice can long endure,
> Raised on a basis insecure?
> Rash mortals, ere you take a wife,
> Contrive your pile to last a life!"

As to the decoration of the interiors of our houses. The walls of the Sitting-rooms can have deal painted, or oak, or mahogany panelling. Or the deal can be painted and stained in a transparent colour and varnished, which gives a very good effect. In rooms where the doors and skirtings, etc., are painted, the mantelpieces should, if in wood, also be painted the same colour. Nothing is in worse taste than to have deal-painted doors and skirtings, etc., with a walnut, oak, or mahogany mantelpiece. Mantelpieces and skirtings are only the survivals of a "treated" panelled room—with the panelling omitted!

The marble mantelpieces and gilt over-glasses of our grandfathers' time were the survivals of the Louis XVI. period, when the walls were treated with plaster panels, the ceilings coved and enriched, and the glass over-mantel formed part of the general scheme of decoration. The decoration was omitted and only coarse mantels and still coarser gilt over-mantels remained.

One word about blinds. Wherever possible, the modern atrocity of the roller-blind should be avoided. With casement windows they are absolutely out of keeping. They collect the dirt, they are expensive to have cleaned, and they are constantly getting out of order. Thin blinds—often called studio curtains—made of a soft stuff, hung on thin iron, brass or copper rods, are the best. In some windows, they can be made in two heights—one set from the top of the window to the transom or meeting-rail, and the other from the transom or meeting-rail down to the cill. These blinds can be obtained in white and in a variety of colours. One great advantage is that they can be easily taken down and washed. Floors should be wax-polished or stained and varnished; and squares of carpets or rugs should be pinned down. These can then be readily taken away and shaken.

Care should be taken, in the smaller type of Houses, that all the fittings and fitments be plain and simple, carving being very seldom, if ever, introduced. Even the door-handles, finger-plates, gas or electric-light fittings should be selected for the simplicity and gracefulness of their designs, rather than for the richness of their effect. Richly—and usually very badly and coarsely—chased finger-plates and door-handles in a simple type of House, always look out of place. As Cowley in "The Wish," says:—" My House a cottage more than Palace, and should fitting be for all my use, not luxury."

With regard to the colours of the painting of the doors, mantels, skirtings, etc.: even in the suburbs of large and manufacturing towns, it is best to have white paint—varnished, if desired. For sanitary reasons, it is better to know the evils that be than not to know them. If the paint is dirty, it is better for you to know it, and then it can be washed. With dark-coloured paints the dirt is not so noticeable, and the woodwork does not therefore get washed so often. Outside doors can be painted in colours and varnished.

And now a word about the Garden. Even with small houses, the designer of the house should design the garden—in any case, that part of it that is adjacent to the house. The man who paints the picture nearly always chooses the frame; and the garden is the frame of the house. Near the house, the garden should always be of a formal character, since it is evident that a house, built with straight square walls, cannot harmonise with curly paths immediately next to it. Formal borders and paths should therefore certainly be arranged immediately around the house, but they can be gradually "shaded off" or "vignetted" into landscape gardens, as they stretch farther from it, if the owner's conceptions lie towards landscape gardens. The charm of the old formal English gardens is in their quietude and simplicity. Note the intense force the dark yew hedges have in throwing up the delicate greens and tints of the flowers. See what a beautiful green the grass is when near a yew tree. Compare the house with its old-fashioned creepers, straight box-edged paths, herbaceous borders, straight square-cut yew hedges and formal beds, with the house surrounded by laurels and monkey trees, with curly paths, beds like centipedes,

PREFACE.

and imitation rock-edged walks! How peaceful is the former and how coarse and vulgar the latter!

Spenser in the "Fairie Queene" sings the praises of the formal garden:—

> "False labyrinths, fond runner's eyes to daze;
> All which by Nature made did Nature self amaze,
> And all without were walks and alleys dight,
> With divers trees enranged in even ranks;
> And here and there were pleasant arbours pight
> And shady seats, and sundry flow'ring banks,
> To sit and rest the walker's weary shanks."

Shady walks, arbours and evenly arranged trees appear to be the key-note to follow when we lay out our gardens. We must also be careful about even the smallest details, such as gates and fences. Excellent terra-cotta vases, copied from those in old Italian Gardens, in which standard trees can be planted, can now be bought in London at a very moderate cost. Lead figures often lend a charm to a garden; Sundials, and perhaps a small Fountain—a basin with a stone curb and a bronze jet being sufficient—all help to make it "a thing of beauty and a joy for ever," where the owner may look around and say with Keats:—

> ". . . . . So will I rest in hope,
> To see wide plains, fai trees and lawney slope;
> The morn, the eve, the light, the shade, the flowers;
> Clear streams, smooth lakes, and overlooking towers."

R. A. BRIGGS.

AMBERLEY HOUSE,
   12, NORFOLK STREET, STRAND, W.C.,
      March, 1904.

DESCRIPTION OF PLATES.

PLATE I. illustrates a House designed to be built at Johannesburg, South Africa. Labour being now very expensive in the Colony, the design has been kept as quiet and as simple as possible. The walls would be built of local bricks and covered externally with "rough-cast," and the roofs would be tiled. Wide verandahs and balconies have been provided almost entirely round the House, to protect from the sun and to keep the rooms as cool as possible.

PLATES II. and III.—These plates illustrate a House that was designed to be built at Wimbledon, at a cost of about £2350, for which tenders were received. The width of the site necessitated the plan being made as compact as possible. The walls would be faced externally with red bricks, the roof being tiled. The woodwork throughout would be painted white, except the front entrance door, which would be of oak, varnished.

PLATES IV. and V. show a House which was built in Aberdeenshire, N.B., at a cost of about £1400. The walls to the ground floor were built of rough local stone. The walls above were of studwork, covered with Norwegian green slates of a small size, and were designed to have a heavy projecting "tilt" to shoot the rain clear of the stone walls. The roof was covered also with Norwegian green slates, but of a larger size. The woodwork throughout was painted white, except the outside doors, which were bright green.

PLATES VI. and VII.—This is a sketch-design for a House, which was built at Welwyn, Herts, with some modifications. Plate VII. shows the entrance front. It was suggested that the whole of the walls should be covered externally with "rough-cast" and distempered a light cream colour, that the roofs should be tiled, and the woodwork throughout should be painted white. The cost of this House, without the upper part of Tower and the "Shell" over door, was about £3100.

PLATES VIII. and IX.—These plates illustrate a House designed to be built in a position where the road is considerably above the level of the site. On the road-level there are the Drawing Room and the Sitting Room Hall, with a staircase giving access to the Dining Room on the lower level of the site; on this lower level are the entrance to the Garden and the Kitchen Offices. Six Bedrooms and a Bathroom are provided. Plate IX. shows the Entrance Front from the road. The walls to the basement and the ground floor will be of rough local stone, those to the ground floor being "rough-cast." The roofs will be covered with green slates.

PLATES X., XI., XII., XIII. and XIV. show the alterations and additions carried out to an old House, 54, Kensington Park Road, Kensington, the walls on the plans shown black being the new work, and those "hatched" being the old work. Plate XI. shows the Entrance Front and Plate XII. the Garden Front. The Gardens, as shown, were laid out in a formal manner. Plate XIII. shows the Hall with the ingle-nook and stairs up to the Library and Billiard Room. The woodwork of the Hall was painted white and varnished. Plate XIV. shows the Library with the fitted book-cases, stone mantelpiece and enriched plaster ceiling.

PLATES XV. and XVI.—This is a design for a small House containing Dining Room, Drawing Room, Sitting Room Hall, four Bedrooms, Bathroom and Kitchen Offices. The ground floor walls, it is suggested, should be of local stone, the walls to the first floor being of studwork covered with small fish-scale-shaped green Norwegian slates. The roof might be slated with square slates and the woodwork painted white

PLATES XVII., XVIII., and XIX. show the plans and the Entrance and Garden Fronts of a House which has been built at Dorking at a cost of between £1500 and £1600. The walls were faced with red bricks, and the roofs were tiled. The woodwork was painted white. Two Attic-Bedrooms were provided in the roof.

PLATE XX.—This is a design for a House in the "Colonial Style." The walls would be built of brick, and covered externally with "rough-cast." The quoins would be of stone. The shutters would be painted bright green. Seven Attic-Bedrooms are provided in the roof, the top of which being flat and surrounded by a balustrade, would afford an opportunity for seeing distant views, if obtainable.

PLATES XXI. and XXII.—These plates show the plans and the Entrance Front of a House to be built, with some modifications, in Scotland. The ground floor walls will be of local stone and the walls above will be of studwork, covered with green slates. The roofs will also be slated. The woodwork will be painted white. Eight Bedrooms and three Dressing Rooms are provided.

PLATE XXIII. shows the plan and View of a Hall and Staircase. The woodwork would be of oak, dull wax-polished.

PLATES XXIV. and XXV. show the plans and the Entrance Front of a House designed to be built at Kingston. Advantage has been taken of the road being considerably above the level of the site, as in Plates VIII. and IX. On the road level are the Entrance and Hall, with staircase giving access to the Drawing Room and Dining Room on the lower level of the site. On this lower floor are also the Kitchen Offices. On the floor, level with the road, are two Bedrooms and Dressing Rooms and Bathroom, separated from the Hall by a glass door and screen. On the floor above are two good-sized Attic-Bedrooms, and a Boxroom. The walls would be built of brick and "rough-cast" externally, the roofs being tiled. The woodwork would be painted white.

PLATES XXVI., XXVII., XXVIII., and XXIX, show the alterations and additions that have been carried out at Battenhall Mount, Worcester. Plate XXVI. shows the plans, the solid black parts being the new work, and the parts "hatched" being the old work. Plate XXVII. shows the external additions of the Music Room, the Sculpture Gallery, and the Tower. The walls were faced with white bricks with stone "dressings," the roofs being covered with green Westmoreland slates. Plate XXVIII. shows the Sculpture Gallery. The front of the Minstrels' Gallery was executed in stone, as was also the bridge. The woodwork to the roof was carried out in oak, and the floor was in marble. Plate XXIX. shows the Music Room, with the stone mantel. The panelling and doors were in oak, the ceiling being in plaster. It was proposed to place an organ at the end of the Music Room, with a small "echo" organ in the gallery of the Tower on the Second Floor. Plate XXX. shows the proposed Library, with the oak-fitted bookcases and mantelpiece.

PLATES XXXI. and XXXII. illustrate a House which was built in Aberdeenshire, N.B., containing Dining Room, Drawing Room, Hall-Sitting Room, five Bedrooms, Bathroom, and Kitchen Offices. The walls to the Ground Floor were built of local stone, the walls to the First Floor being of studwork covered with slates. The roofs were slated. The woodwork was throughout stained dark brown and oiled. The cost of the House was about £1300.

PLATE XXXIII.—This is a design for a House to be built at Marlow. It was proposed that the walls should be "rough-cast," the gables being of "half-timber" work, and the roofs tiled. A large Parlour, a small Boudoir, four Bedrooms, Bathroom, and Kitchen Offices are provided.

PLATES XXXIV. and XXXV. show the plans and the Garden Front of a House that has been built near Horley, Surrey, at a cost of about £2500. The walls were built of brick, those to the Ground Floor being faced with red bricks, and those to the First Floor being covered with rough-cast and tiles. The roofs were tiled. The woodwork was painted white throughout.

PLATE XXXVI. shows a design for a Dining Room, the whole of the woodwork being of oak and the ceiling of enriched plaster. The frieze above the panelling was covered with Japanese paper cut into squares, each square being nailed to the wall with brass-headed nails.

PLATES XXXVII. and XXXVIII. show the plans and the Entrance Front of a House that was proposed to be built in Scotland. The walls would be of brick, faced externally on the Ground Floor with stone and above with "rough-cast." The roofs would be slated. The woodwork would be painted white, except the louvre shutters, which would be bright green. Five Attic Bedrooms are provided on the Second Floor.

PLATES XXXIX. and XL.—This is a design for a House in the South African Colonial style, the plans made being suitable to those Colonies. The walls would be "rough-cast" externally, and the woodwork would be painted white.

PLATES XLI. and XLII.—These plates show how an old Windmill has been converted into a Dwelling House. The old Mill provided a Dining Room, three Bedrooms, and a Smoking Room in the roof, all of which were circular on plan. A new staircase was built to give access to these rooms. A Bathroom was built on the First Floor. A Parlour, illustrated by Plate XLII., was built on one side of the old Mill, and Kitchen Offices on the other side. The walls of the new work were "rough-cast" on the outside, and the roofs were tiled with local tiles. The Parlour has an open timber roof, and is panelled in oak.

PLATES XLIII. and XLIV.—These illustrations show the Entrance and Garden Fronts of a House which was built, with some modifications, at a cost of about £2300, near Beaulieu, Hants. The two corridors on each side of the Sitting Room, the covered Verandah, and three rooms were omitted, and the Bay Windows towards the garden were built octagonal on plan instead of circular. The gables were slightly altered, copings being introduced in lieu of the verges. The walls were covered with rough-cast, and the roofs were tiled. The woodwork throughout was painted white, except the lower shutters, which were painted bright green.

PLATE XLV.—This House has been erected at Wormley, near Broxbourne, Herts, on a site containing magnificent views, and encircled by a luxuriant belt of trees. In designing this House the aim was to keep it as simple as possible, and to gain the effect more by the treatment of its natural projections than by introducing ornament. As will be seen by the plan, a wide passage was taken the whole length of the house on the First Floor, and at each end were windows for continuous ventilation, forming a veritable *lung* to the House. The wide terrace is protected on the East by the projecting wing and verandah. The cost of the House was about £4200. The walls were faced with red bricks and the roofs were tiled, the woodwork being painted white throughout. The Staircase and the doors to Reception Rooms were of mahogany.

PLATES XLVI., XLVII., and XLVIII.—Plate XLVI. shows the front towards the road of a House with Stables that is being built at Abinger Common, Surrey, at a cost of about £2500, inclusive of the oak panellings, &c. in hall and parlour. These rooms are illustrated by Plates XLVII. and XLVIII.. The walls outside are, up to the First Floor level, faced with red bricks. Above that level the walls to the House are hung with red tiles, and to the stable "rough-cast." The gables to the House have half-timber work, and the gables to the stables have tiles. The whole of the roof is tiled. The woodwork will be covered with "carbolineum." The oak-work outside will be oiled, and inside it will be dull wax-polished.

PLATE XLIX.—This illustration shows the Garden Front of a House which has just been completed at Drumlyn, Moyallon, co. Down, Ireland. It is situated on a beautiful site with fine and extended views towards the South. Bow windows have therefore been introduced in the South and West fronts of the House, so that these views may be thoroughly appreciated from the various rooms. The walls outside are rough-cast, and the roofs are slated with green Westmoreland slates. The shutters are painted green, and the rest of the woodwork in deal has been painted white. The staircase is of oak, and the entrance door and hood are of teak. The Dining Room and Drawing Room have their walls divided up into panelling with mouldings, and are painted cream colour. The cost of this House was about £3800. The garden is now being formed on the lines suggested in the illustration.

DESCRIPTION OF PLATES.

PLATES L. and LI.—Plate L. shows the Entrance Front of a House which has lately been built at Speldhurst, near Tunbridge Wells, Kent, at a cost of about £2100. The walls up to the First Floor level were faced with red bricks, and above that level were tiled. The roof also was tiled. The woodwork to the doors, except the front door which was of oak, and the windows, were painted white. The ceiling to the Hall-Billiard Room and Dining Room have the rafters exposed, filleted and sound-boarded, which have all been covered with "carbolineum." Plate LI. shows a view in the Hall-Billiard Room.

PLATE LII.—This is an illustration of a cheap and effective House designed in the "Colonial" style. The Hall, being carried up two storeys, gives a very light appearance and well ventilated *lung* to the House. It is suggested that the walls should be of rough-cast, and the quoins of red brick. The roof might be either slated with green slates or tiled. The woodwork should be painted white, except the shutters, which might be bright green or violet.

PLATE LIII.—This House has been built at Ewhurst, near Cranleigh, Surrey, at a cost of about £1500. The walls up to the First Floor level were faced with red bricks, and above that level were tiled. The roof was also tiled. The woodwork throughout was stained dark brown, and covered with boiled linseed oil.

PLATE LIV. and FRONTISPIECE.—These Plates show the Plans and Garden Front of a House that was proposed to be built in Surrey, with its walls rough-cast and its roof covered with thatch. The woodwork would have been painted white throughout.

Plate II.

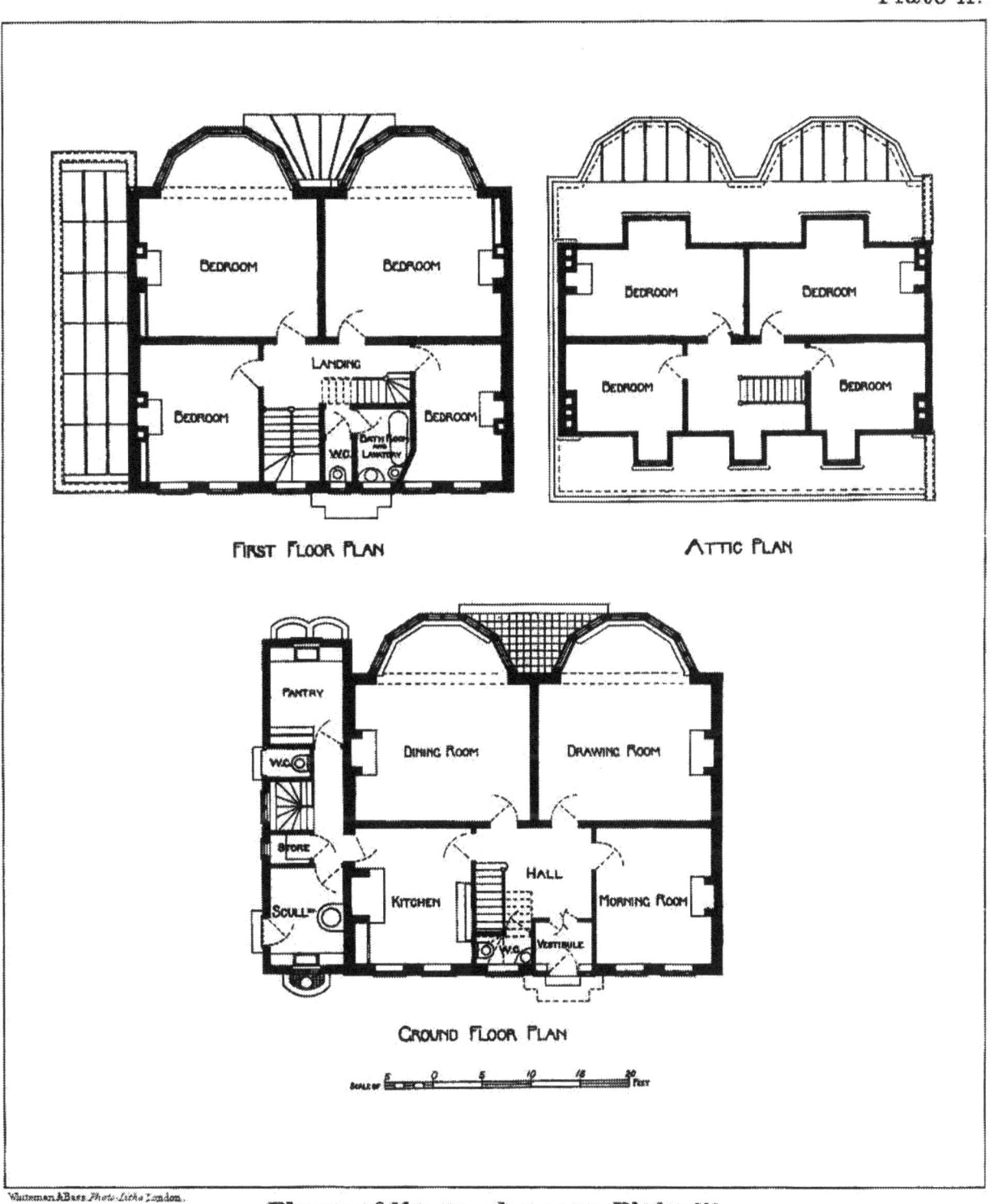

Plans of House shown on Plate III.

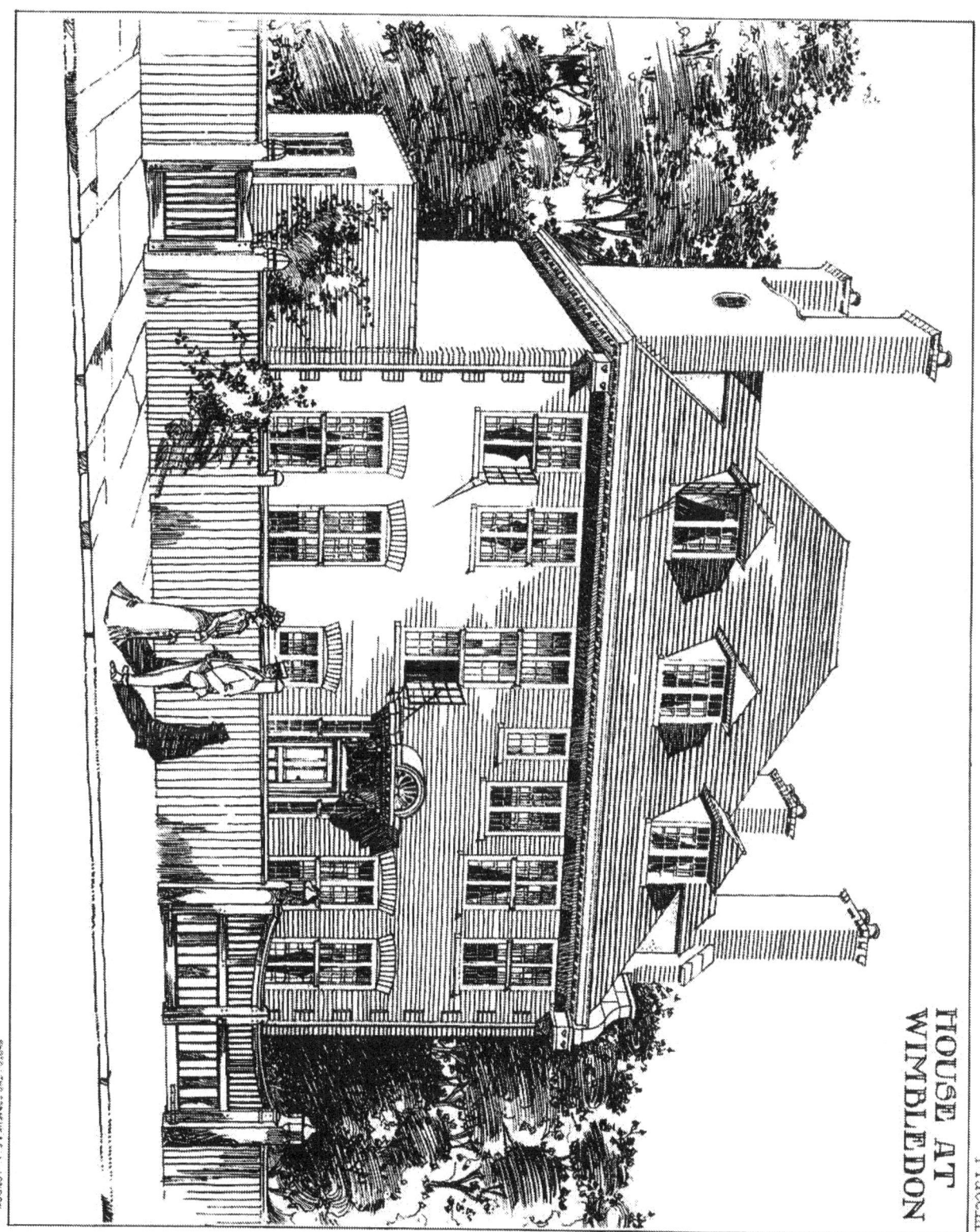

HOUSE AT WIMBLEDON

Plate II

Plate IV.

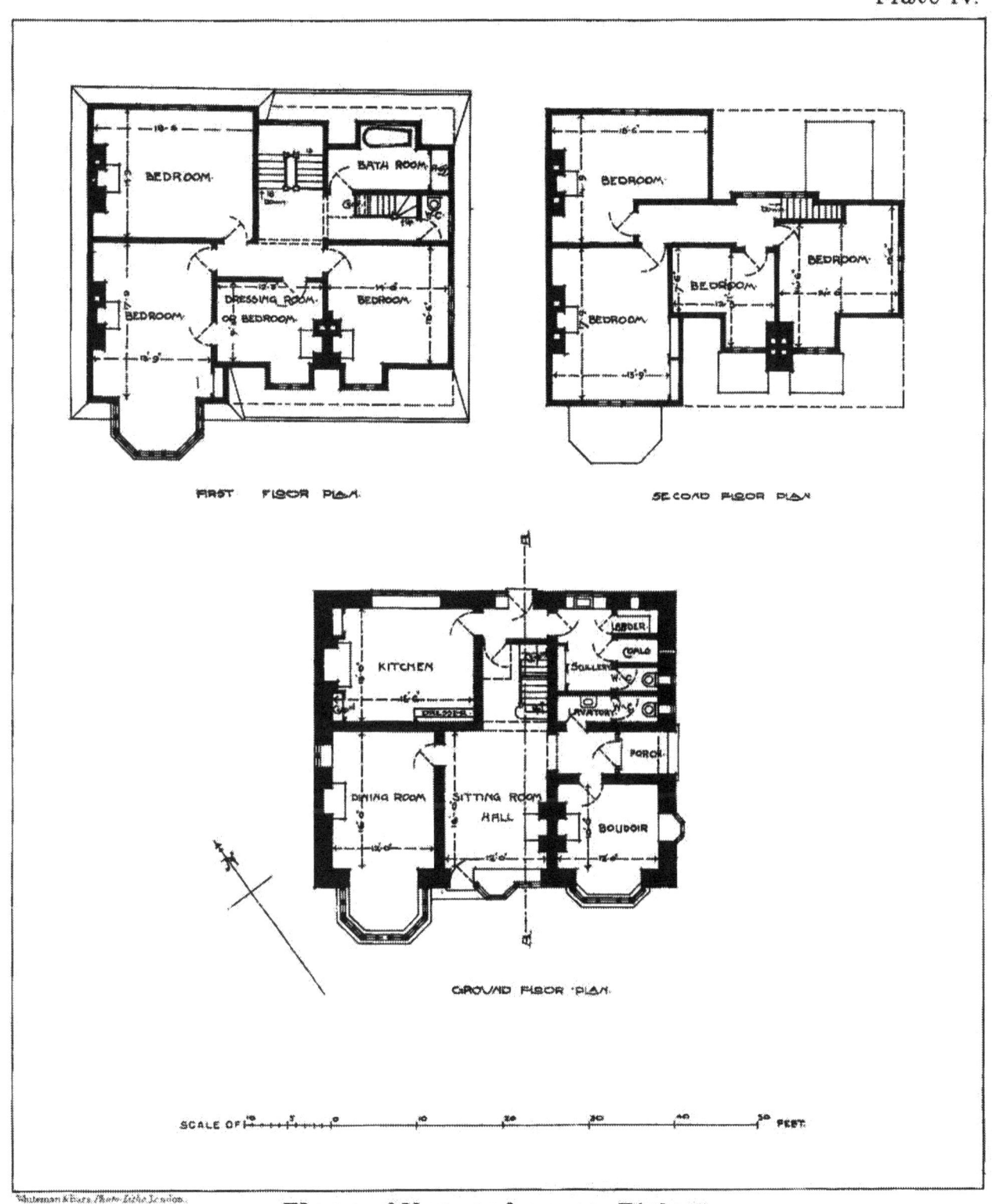

Plans of House shown on Plate V.

HOUSE AT TILLIEFOURE
ABERDEENSHIRE N.B.

Plate VI.

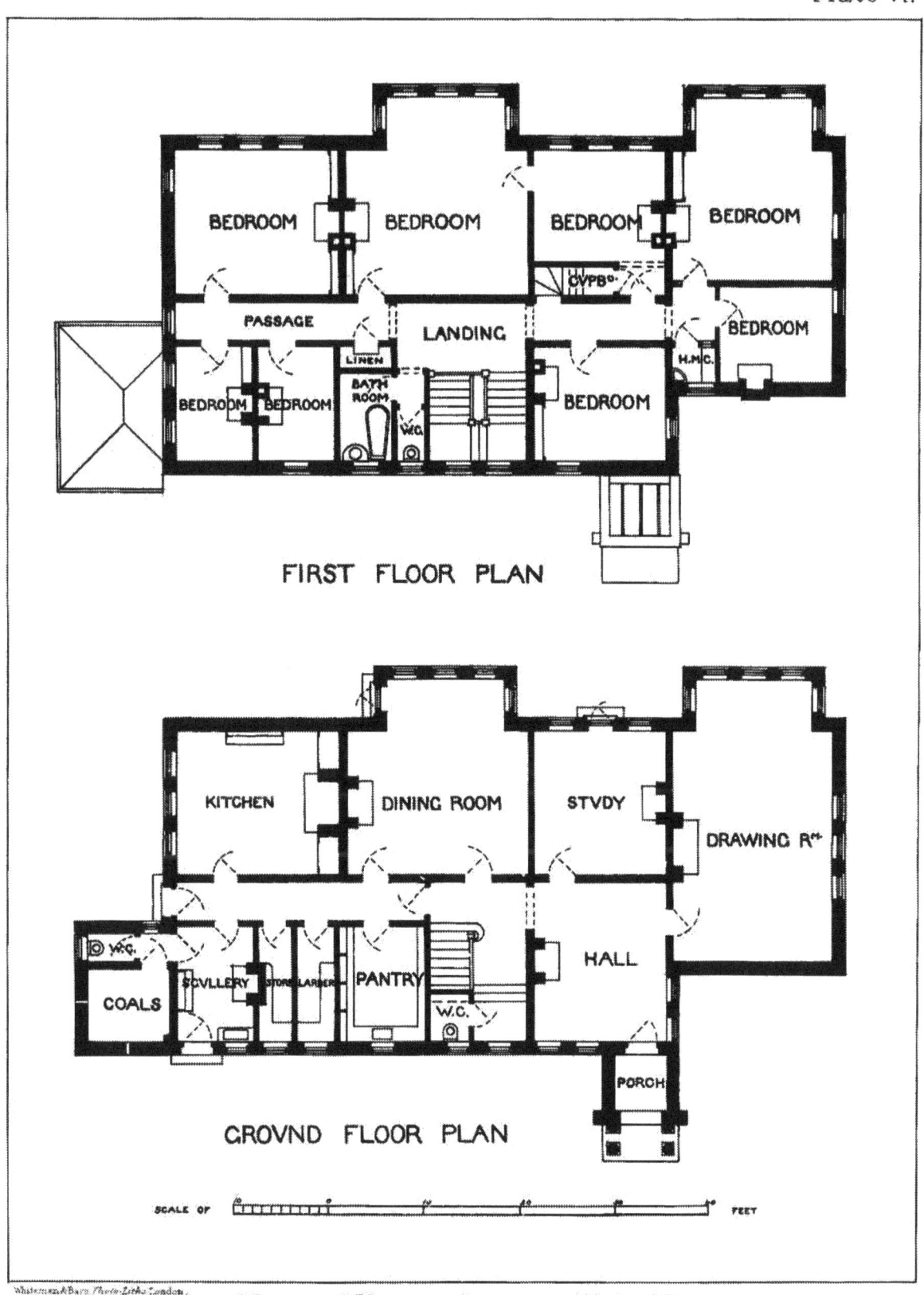

Plans of House shown on Plate VII.

Plate VII

Plate VIII.

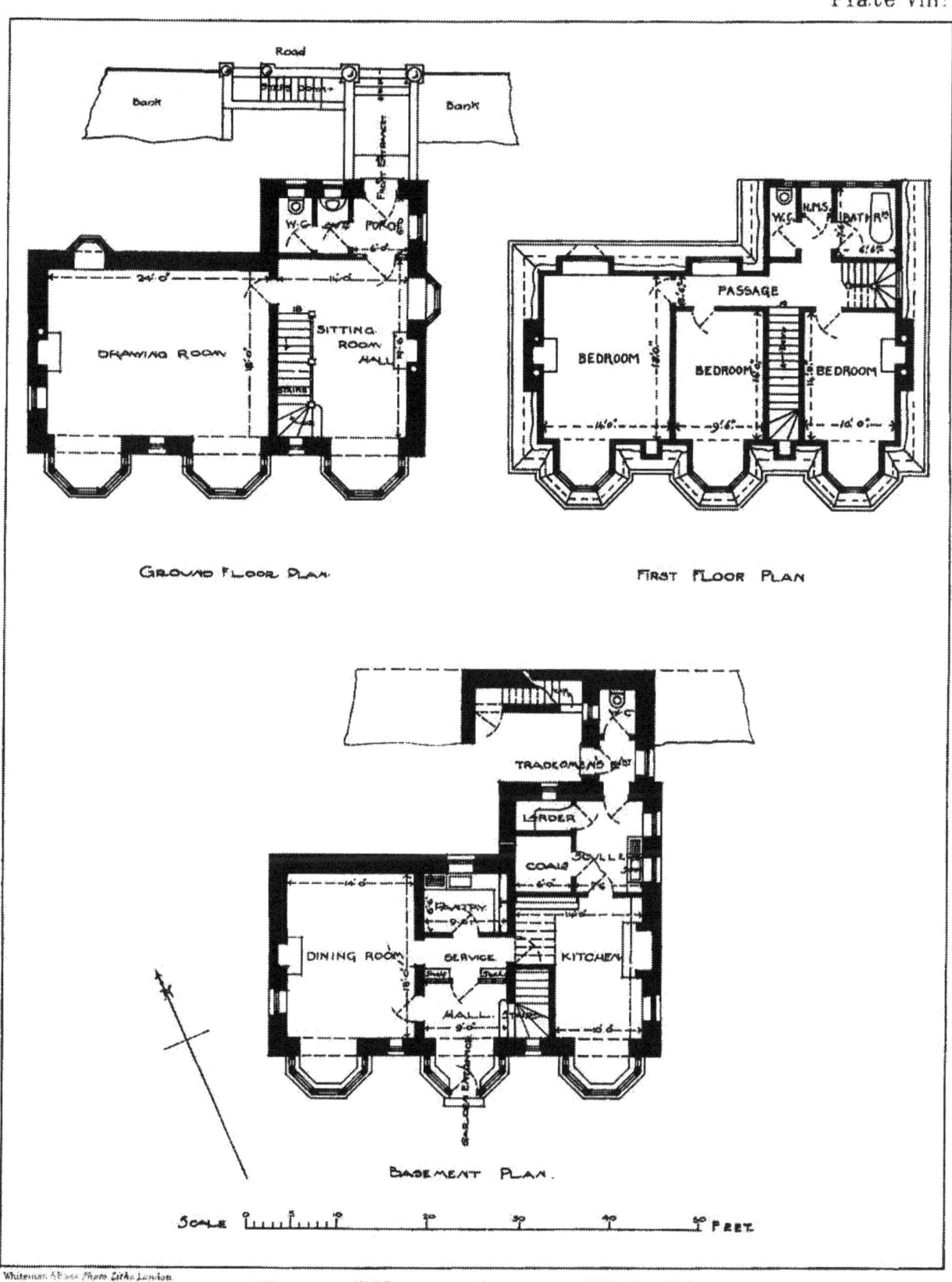

Plans of House shown on Plate IX.

Plate IX

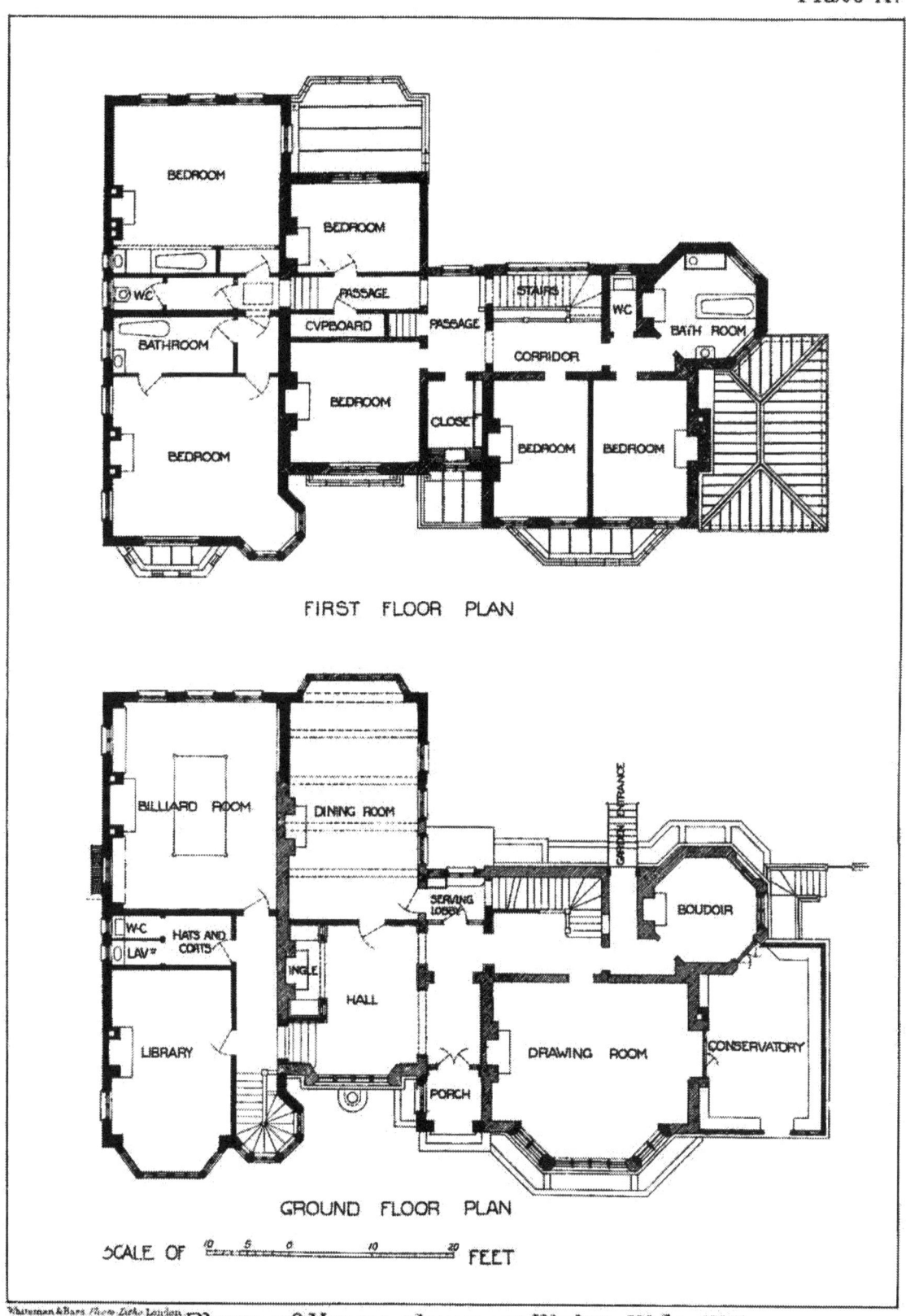

Plate X.

Plans of House shown on Plates XI to XIV.

Plate XI.

Plate XII.

34 KENSINGTON PARK ROAD·W

VIEW in HALL

Plate XIII.

54 Kensington Park Road. W

View in Library

Plate XIV.

Plans of House shown on Plate XVI.

Plate XV.

Plate XVI

Plate XVII.

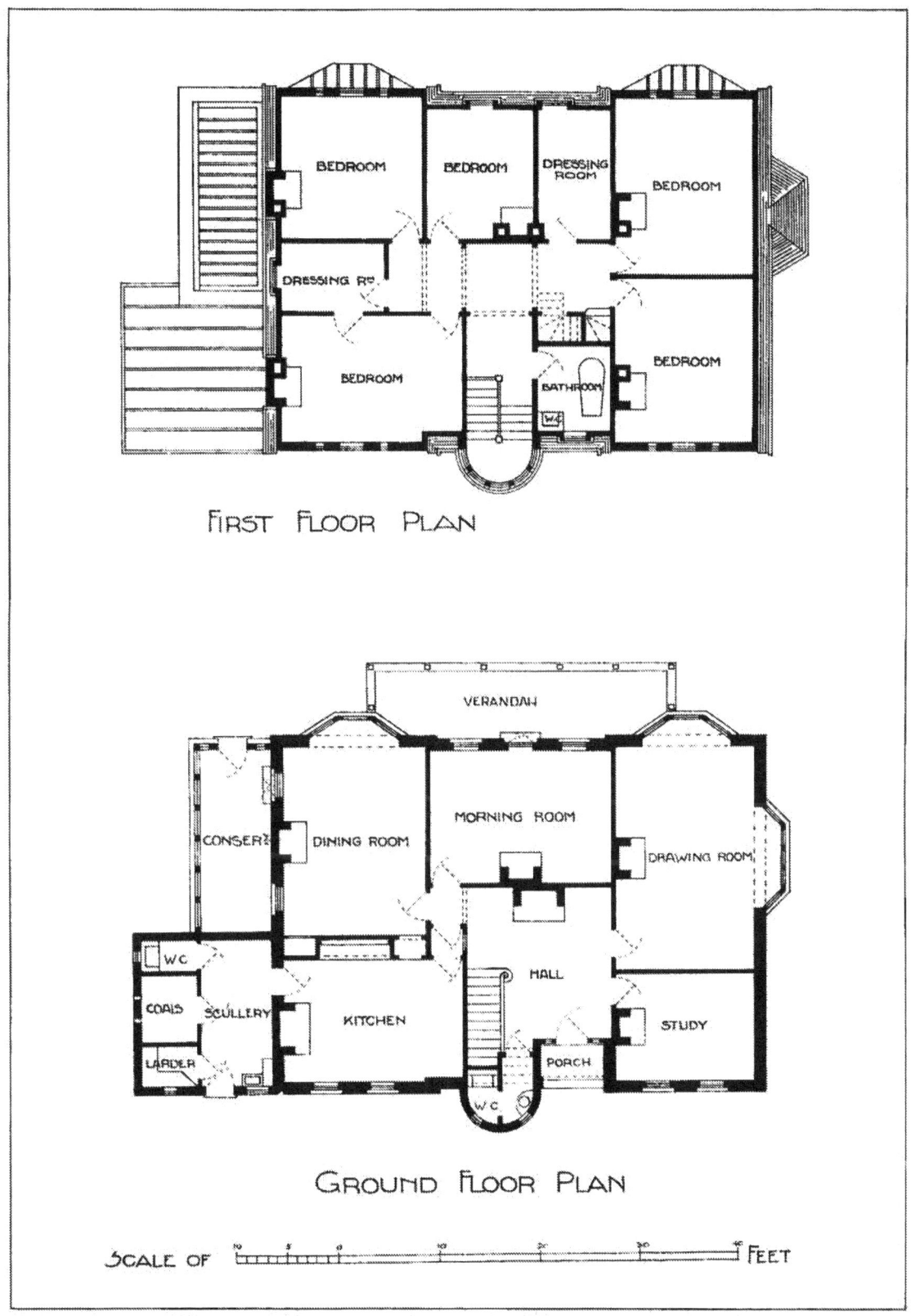

Plans of House shown on Plates XVIII & XIX.

HOUSE AT DORKING
ENTRANCE FRONT

Plate XVII

HOUSE AT DORKING
GARDEN FRONT

Plate XIX

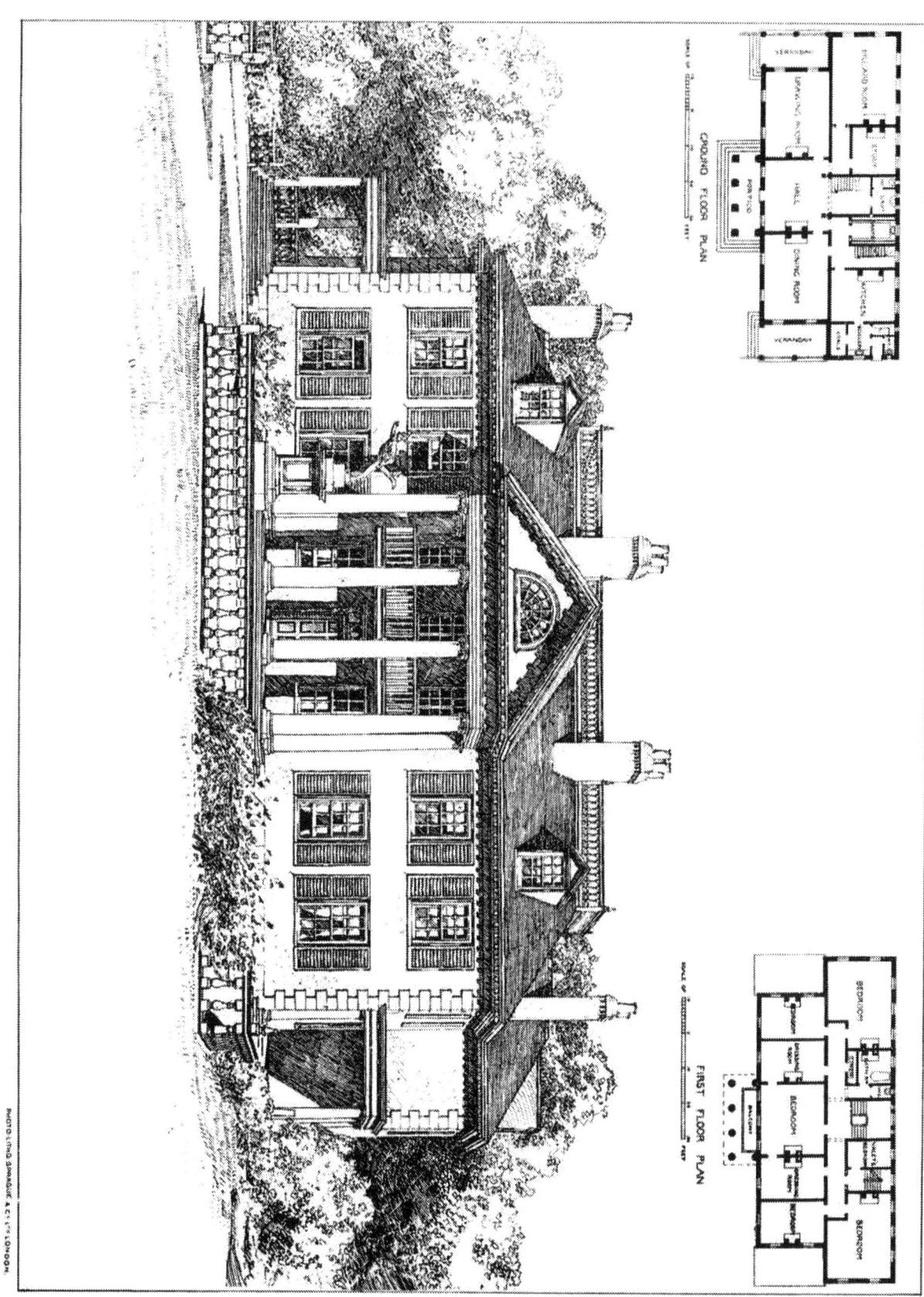

Plate XX

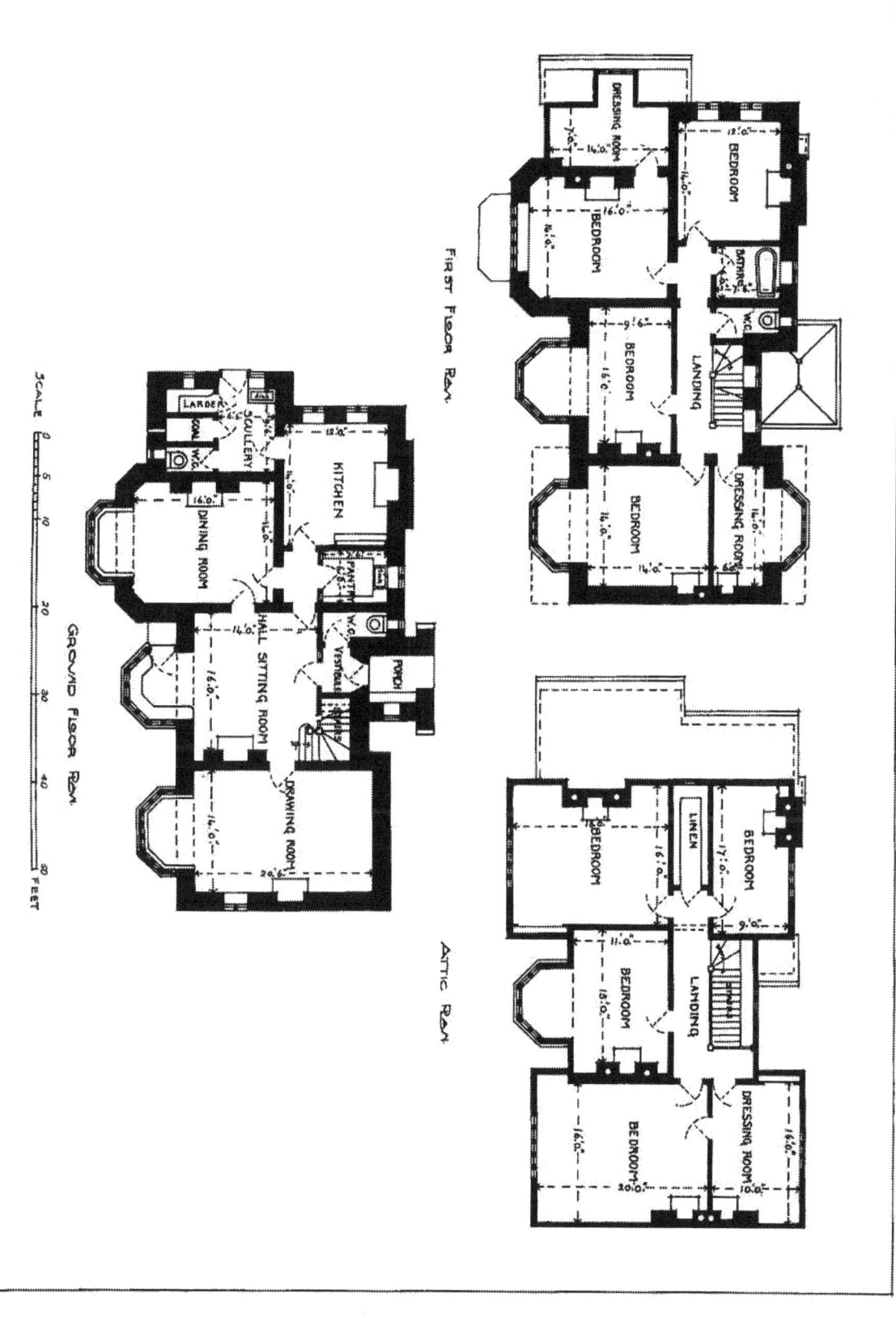

Plans of House shown on Plate XXII.

Plate XII

Plate XXIII.

Plans of House shown on Plate XXV.

GROUND FLOOR PLAN

FIRST FLOOR PLAN

Plate XXIV.

PROPOSED HOUSE AT KINGSTON
FRONT TOWARDS ROAD

Plate XXV.

Plans of House shown on Plates XXVII to XXX.

GROUND FLOOR PLAN

FIRST FLOOR PLAN

Plate XXVI.

ADDITIONS TO BATTENHALL MOUNT
WORCESTER

Plate XXVII.

Plate XXVIII.

Plate XXIX

BATTENHALL MOUNT
WORCESTER

VIEW IN LIBRARY

Plate XXX.

Plate XXXI.

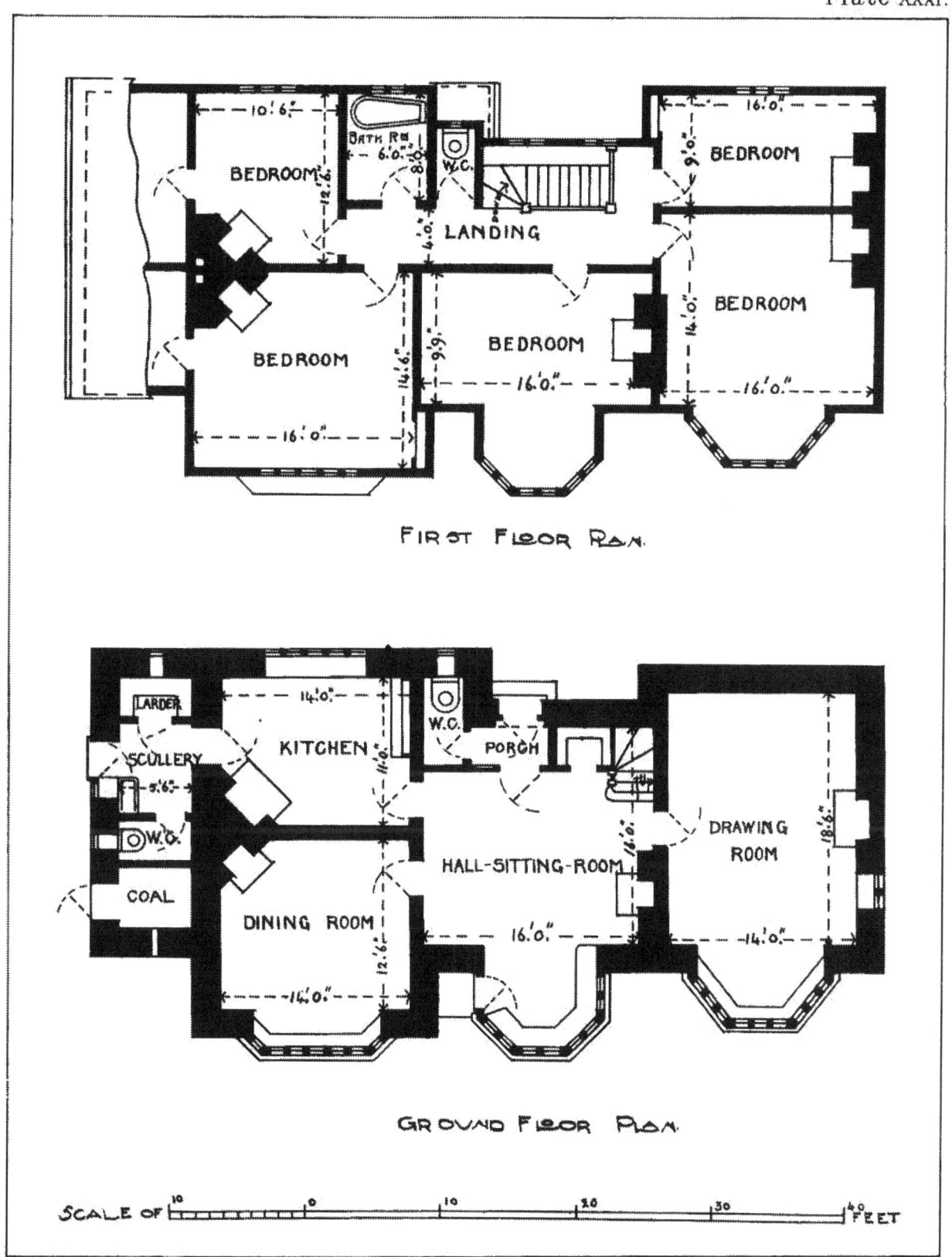

Plans of House shown on Plate XXXII.

Plate XXXIII

Plate XXXIV

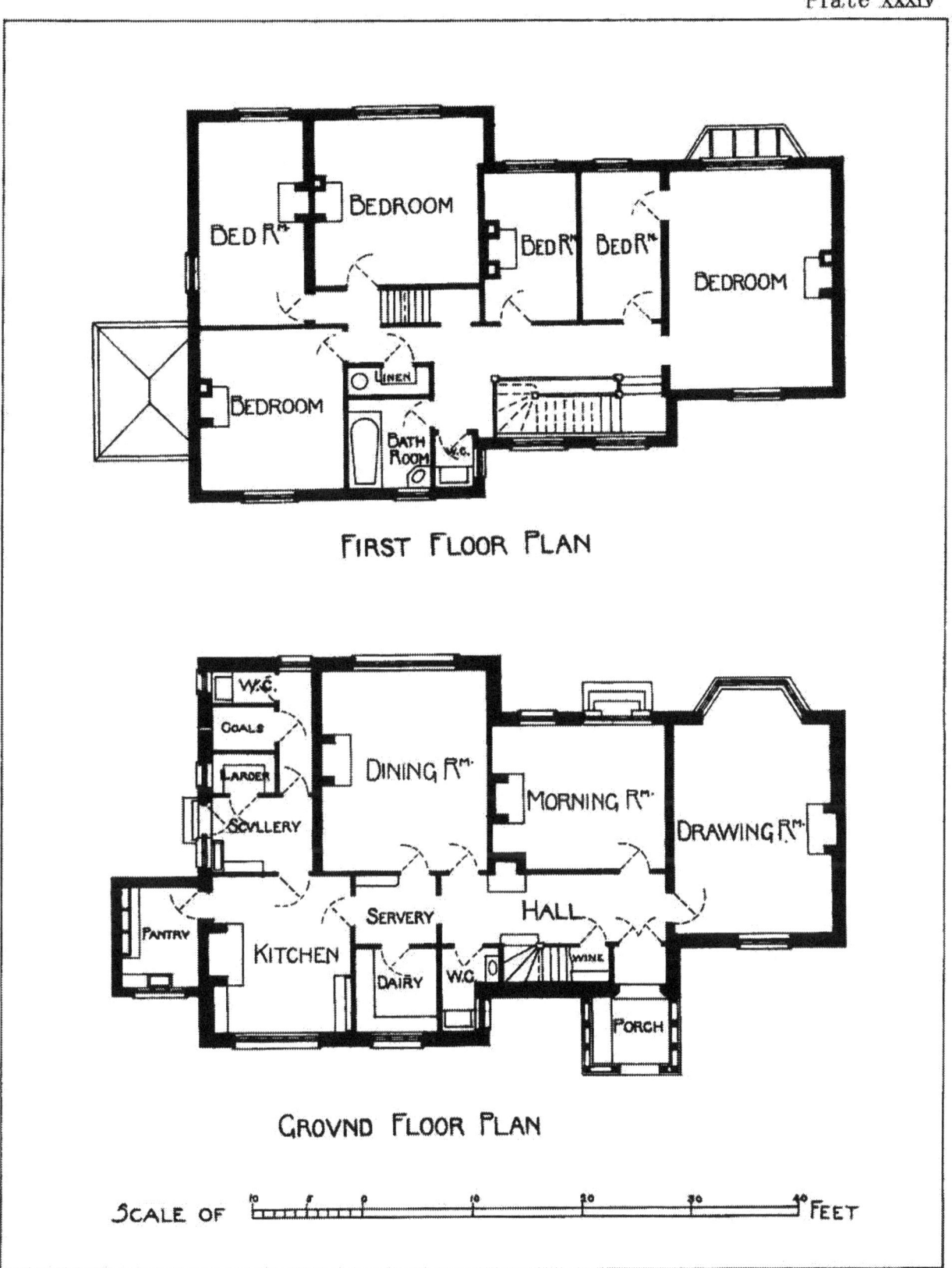

Plans of House shown on Plate XXXV.

HOUSE AT HORLEY
GARDEN FRONT

Plate XXXVI

Plans of House shown on Plate XXXVIII.

GROUND FLOOR PLAN.
- Scullery
- Kitchen
- Pantry
- Hall
- Dining Room
- Drawing Room
- Library

FIRST FLOOR PLAN.
- Bath Room
- Bedroom
- Bedroom
- Dressing Room
- Bedroom

SECOND FLOOR PLAN.
- Dressing Room
- Bedroom
- Bedroom
- Bedroom
- Bedroom

SCALE FEET

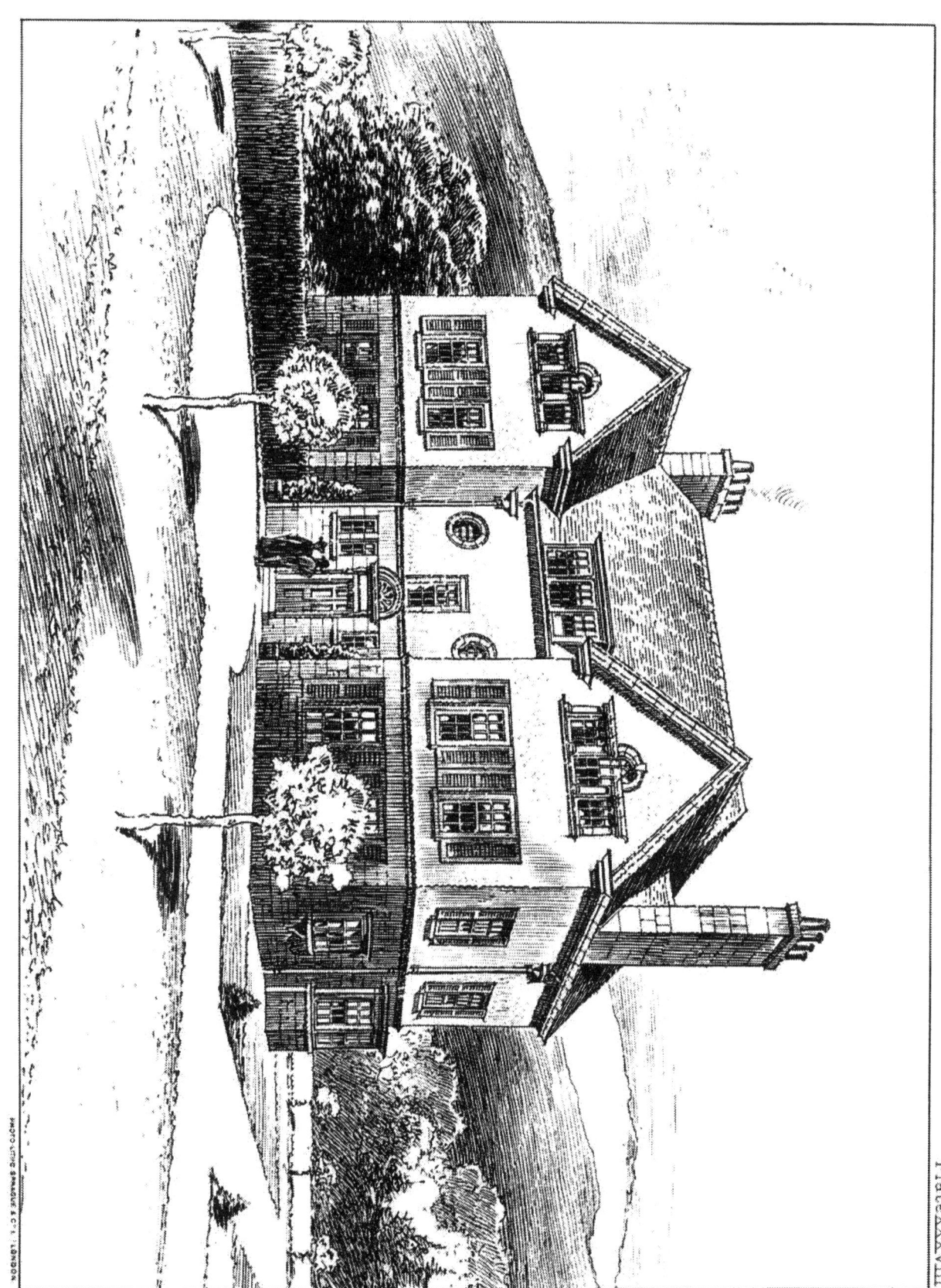

Plate XXXVII

Plans of House shown on Plate XL.

Plate XXXIX.

Plate XI.

Addition to The Old Mill, Alvechurch.

Plate XI.

Plate XLII.

The Parlour
Old Mill
Aldeburgh

Plate XLIV.

MANOR HOUSE, WORMLEY.
GARDEN FRONT.

Plate XLV.

HOUSE – ABINGER COMMON
VIEW IN HALL

Plate XVII.

HOUSE at ABINGER COMMON

VIEW IN PARLOUR

Plate XLviii.

Plate XLIX.

HOUSE AT SPELDHURST
VIEW IN HALL

Plate III.

HOUSE AT EWHURST.

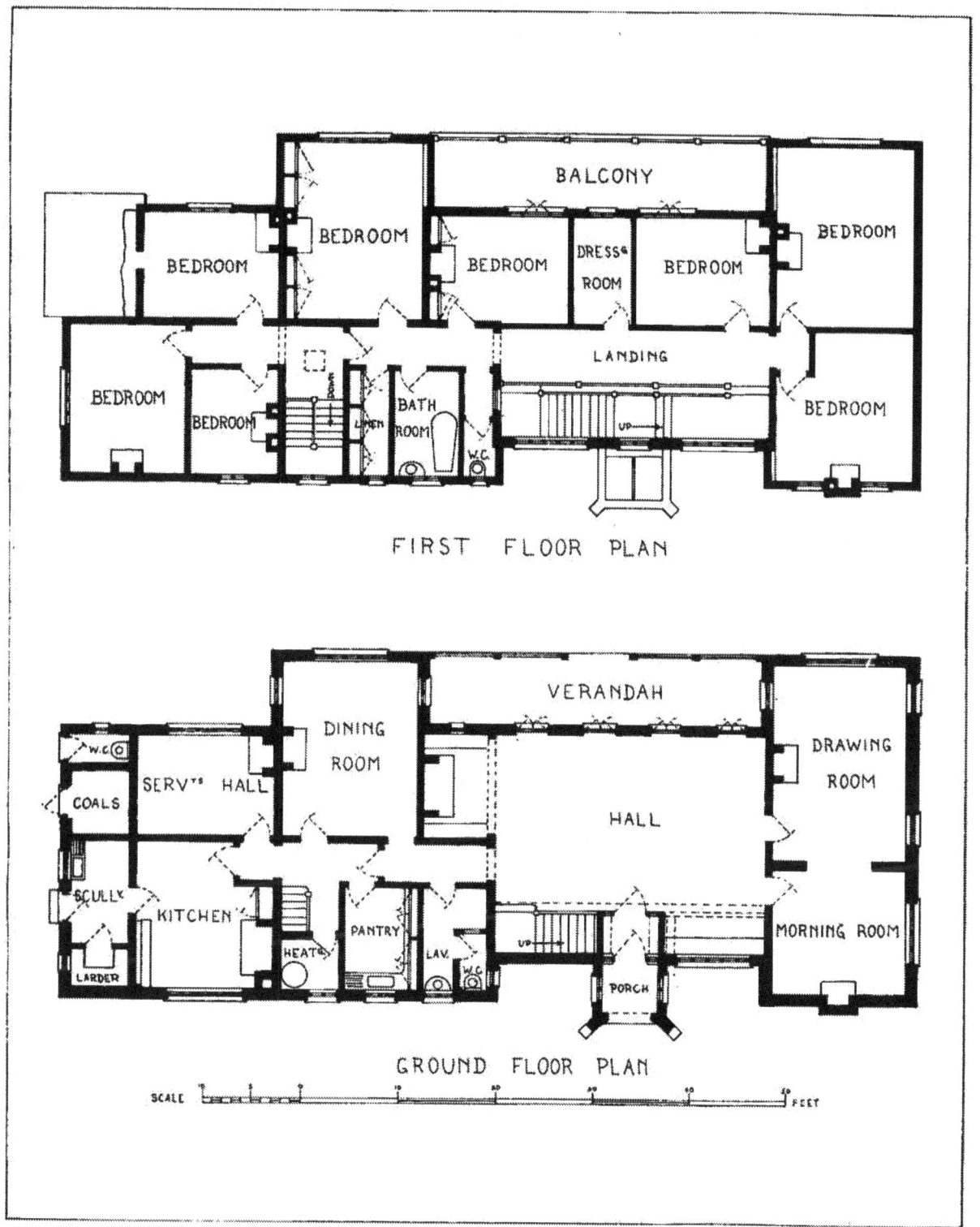

Plate LIV.

FIRST FLOOR PLAN

GROUND FLOOR PLAN

www.ingramcontent.com/pod-product-compliance
Lightning Source LLC
Chambersburg PA
CBHW080346170426
43194CB00014B/2702